# make your small business thrive

Kevin Duncan

For UK order enquiries: please contact Bookpoint Ltd, 130 Milton Park, Abingdon, Oxon OX14 4SB. *Telephone*: +44 (0) 1235 827720. *Fax*: +44 (0) 1235 400454. Lines are open 09.00–17.00, Monday to Saturday, with a 24-hour message answering service. Details about our titles and how to order are available at www.hoddereducation.com

*British Library Cataloguing in Publication Data*: a catalogue record for this title is available from the British Library.

Copyright © 2011 Kevin Duncan

*In UK*: All rights reserved. Apart from any permitted use under UK copyright law, no part of this publication may be reproduced or transmitted in any form or by any means, electronic or mechanical, including photocopy, recording, or any information, storage and retrieval system, without permission in writing from the publisher or under licence from the Copyright Licensing Agency Limited. Further details of such licences (for reprographic reproduction) may be obtained from the Copyright Licensing Agency Limited, of Saffron House, 6–10 Kirby Street, London EC1N 8TS.

Typeset by MPS Limited, a Macmillan Company.

Printed in Great Britain for Hodder Education, an Hachette UK Company, 338 Euston Road, London NW1 3BH, by CPI Cox & Wyman, Reading, Berkshire RG1 8EX.

The publisher has used its best endeavours to ensure that the URLs for external websites referred to in this book are correct and active at the time of going to press. However, the publisher and the author have no responsibility for the websites and can make no guarantee that a site will remain live or that the content will remain relevant, decent or appropriate.

Hachette UK's policy is to use papers that are natural, renewable and recyclable products and made from wood grown in sustainable forests. The logging and manufacturing processes are expected to conform to the environmental regulations of the country of origin.

| Impression number | 10 9 8 7 6 5 4 3 2 |
| Year | 2015 2014 2013 2012 2011 |

*Dedicated to my daughters, Rosanna and Shaunagh, and my wife Sarah, the Sleeping Lion.*

Kevin Duncan worked in advertising and direct marketing for twenty years. For the last ten years he has worked on his own as a business adviser, marketing expert and author. He advises various businesses as a non-executive director, business strategist and trainer.

kevinduncan@expertadvice.co.uk
expertadviceonline.com

Also by Kevin Duncan:
*Business Greatest Hits*
*Marketing Greatest Hits*
*Run Your Own Business*
*Small Business Survival*
*So What?*
*Start*
*Tick Achieve*

# Contents

| | | |
|---|---|---|
| 1 | So your business is under pressure. What now? | 2 |
| 2 | Are you disciplined enough to survive? | 10 |
| 3 | Thinking is free | 22 |
| 4 | Thinking stage 1: what are the facts? | 32 |
| 5 | Thinking stage 2: what's your own opinion? | 44 |
| 6 | Set up your business tripwires and grenades | 56 |
| 7 | Write your own Lifesmile Statement | 68 |
| 8 | Don't confuse movement with progress | 76 |
| 9 | Corporations don't have memories | 86 |

# 1

# *so your business is under pressure. What now?*

Don't panic. Things go wrong in business all the time. Pause to think carefully, stay calm, and take advice if necessary. Then decide what to do. Don't get too formulaic about survival and growth. Life's a mess. Adapt. Change something, and do it fast. It's time for tough love and some tough thinking. Don't dodge the facts, and don't kid yourself. You need a warts and all appraisal of your trading conditions, coupled with appropriate remedies. Ask yourself some tough questions. The tougher the better. Put yourself and your business right under the microscope. If you can't be ruthless enough, get someone else to interrogate you. All those things you think are vital and take for granted in your business: so what? It sounds like a dismissive question but that's the point. There may be a case for thinking again.

## What to do when things go wrong

It's a tricky business. What exactly do you do when your business is not going as you wish? Difficult times require difficult decisions, based on solid thinking. Panicking is no use, and nor is fruitless worrying. So don't rush into a blue funk and assume that the world is ending. Stay calm and review your business and your options as coolly as you possibly can, even if you are not happy with the circumstances. Stick to the facts and be as objective as possible. Check with respected friends or partners whether your thinking is veering off into strange areas, and take heed of their wise words to self-correct.

## You cannot be prescriptive about survival or growth

Although this book contains advice, it does not attempt to prescribe exactly how your business can survive or grow by following a fixed pattern. You need to be open-minded, and cherry-pick the ideas that best suit your circumstances. Growth in particular is always an adventure, and it needs to be viewed as such, and approached with the right attitude.

**'An adventure is an inconvenience rightly considered.'**

G. K. Chesterton

Rushing into the unknown is all part of the thrill of running a business. It is all a bit of an adventure. Some people love it. Some crave it. Some find themselves in charge of businesses but didn't necessarily ask to be there. Businesses always have issues and problems. You can't have customers without having to sort out a lot of tricky stuff. You can't have staff without having to maintain them. So let's assume that you are in charge of a business. It doesn't matter whether you set it up yourself, or whether someone else did. The point is, it has been up and running for a while, and the launch phase is complete. The business is established. So what are you going to do now?

# Time for tough love and some tough thinking

You'll have heard of tough love, when people need to be told the truth for their own good. Well now's the time for some tough thinking. That means more confrontation. Not with other people, but with the conflicting thoughts in your head. This tough thinking may apply to you personally, or to your business, and this book contains ways to approach both areas, because they are always interlinked. It is time to confront your demons. This is the basic dilemma all businesses face when they have set up, and have then paused to reflect or have become restless. Let's start with a series of nasty questions that require candid answers. If you think you are not going to like some of the answers, then take some quiet time out and don't attempt the process when you are at work. And please, don't lie to yourself – it renders the whole exercise pointless and you are a grown-up now! Okay, take a deep breath.

## Some nasty questions

* Are you happy?
* Are you in charge of your own destiny?
* Are you king of nothing?
* Are you proud of what you have achieved?
* Are you impressed with yourself?
* Are you status conscious?
* Are you out of your depth?
* Where does it all end?
* When does it all end?

What sort of answers have you come up with? This is not a psychological test, so there are no right and wrong ones, but what is the general shape? If you are essentially happy, and in charge of your own destiny, then you might as well stop reading this and go out for a celebratory meal immediately. If you conclude that you are king of nothing, then there is something wrong. If you find yourself in a top role purely for status reasons, or if

*1 so your business is under pressure. What now?*          **5**

you feel out of your depth, then we certainly have some work to do. If you have no idea when or where the whole thing is going to end, don't panic. That might not be the end of the world, but it is preferable if you can answer one or the other of them. If you can picture where it is all going to end, but not when, that's a good start because you know what you want but aren't too concerned about the immediate time frame. If you can envisage when you are going to conclude this thing, but not necessarily where, that could be okay. If you are not sure of either, some thought is required.

In another of my other books I extol the virtues of asking yourself simple questions and being brutally honest about the answers. One of the most powerful of these is: So what? Although potentially annoying if addressed to someone else, it is a great leveller when you ask it of yourself. Try some of these for size (for over 200 more, read my book, *So What?*).

## Some so what? questions

* You're in charge. So what?
* You have lots of people reporting to you. So what?
* You have a large office. So what?
* You have your name on the door. So what?
* You are your own boss. So what?
* You earn more money than before. So what?
* Your sales are up this year. So what?
* Your profit is up on last year. So what?

You get the idea. There is no right or wrong answer, but hopefully you have stirred yourself up a bit. The knack is not to give any particular answer, but to know *why* you have given that answer. If you do know why, and are happy with that response, then excellent. If you are not happy with any particular answer, then you have some thinking to do on that topic. Once you get the hang of it, you can invent your own questions, so long as they are all personal to you, and so long as all the responses that you give are honest. Do not fall into the trap of self-delusion.

# Can't get no satisfaction

Most people who run businesses are never quite satisfied, because they always feel they have unfinished business, no matter how well things are going. There's always something else that can be done. They are constantly dealing with an unfinished article. They may also be dealing with post-launch blues, or going through a three-year itch. 'Three-year itch' is of course a catch-all phrase for any kind of period of dissatisfaction, and the timing of it varies hugely. For some it is three months, for some seven years, and for some it never comes at all. But if it does, it can eat away as insidious self-doubt, and it needs to be confronted urgently before it starts to ruin everything – that is the business and your sanity.

> **'Self-pity is the enemy of generosity.'**
>
> Alexander Chancellor

So what happens if you discover that, on reflection, you are not that happy with your state of affairs? Well, you have got some work to do. There is no room for self-pity here. Your friends and family won't enjoy it, nor will your staff if you have them and, ultimately, it is of no use to you either. So you need to understand why you are not happy, and set about trying to fix it.

> **'Do not weep; do not wax indignant. Understand.'**
>
> Baruch Spinoza

The key to this is *understanding*. There is no point sitting around bewailing the fact that things are as they are, when you could be spending time working out why they are as they are. Therein lies the potential to change things. Get to the heart of the matter, and concentrate on which bits you can influence personally, and who can help you attend to the rest. It is the solution you are after, not the waffle and preamble that takes you longer to get there. So spot the endgame, and head for that point straightaway.

> **'Almost every man wastes part of his life in attempts to display qualities that he does not possess.'**
>
> Samuel Johnson

*1  so your business is under pressure. What now?*

Part of the reason may be that you are trying to do things that you do not enjoy, or that you are not particularly good at. There is no disgrace in not being brilliant at everything. In fact, there is barely anyone alive who is. So don't beat yourself up about it. Instead work out ways to circumnavigate areas that don't suit you, re-engineer the business so that you don't have to do them, or get other people in to do them for you. That might be staff, or one-off experts. Have a look at Chapters 4 and 5 for effective ways to tackle this area.

> **'Even in slight things, the experience of the new is rarely without some stirring of foreboding.'**
>
> Eric Hoffer

A lot of people do not like change. Indeed, they are often scared of it. There is nothing wrong with that feeling. So long as you don't allow it to be so overwhelming that it genuinely prevents you from any sort of forward motion. If you run your own business, you should be keen to move ever onward. If you run someone else's, equally you will not want to be doing the same thing all the time, so plunge in to the new with a sense of adventure. You might surprise yourself.

## *Flashback*

* Are you being too prescriptive about your survival and growth plans?
* Have you decided what to do next?
* Do you regard the next step as an adventure?
* Have you asked yourself the tricky questions?
* Have you confronted the answers you didn't like?
* Have you thoroughly understood why things are as they are?
* Do you know what you are going to do to make things better?
* Have you eliminated any self-pity?
* Have you found solutions to cover for qualities you do not have?
* Have you braced yourself for some tough thinking?

## Success Story: Amy Watson, the IT supplier who got it just right

Greed and 'world domination' expansion plans can be the death of many a business. Amy knew this, and made sure that her growth plans were based on sound judgement rather than hubris. She had stood in bars with enough boastful businessmen to realize that talking big is only half the story. The phrase 'turnover is vanity, profit is sanity' was one of her favourites.

Amy ran an Information Technology training business, teaching people how to use all the new software packages that came onto the market. Developments were so rapid that there was always a good pipeline of people who needed to update their skills in this area. This forward motion was always tempered, however, by the natural inertia of human nature, and the fact that training is usually one of the first things to be cut or frozen when times get hard.

Amy did her launch research brilliantly, highlighting two top markets for her services: the financial industry for accounting-based software, and the creative industries for artistic, graphics-based software. She trained herself on the whole lot first and marketed herself to the relevant companies. After a year, when her personal time was almost fully booked, she recruited an expert in each category on a freelance basis to help. They were delighted to have the work and she did not want them on a payroll.

After three years, she had a pool of ten such freelancers, the knack being that they were only paid if she was. She then had enough in the bank to hire a low-cost room in which to hold the training. This was part of her plan to increase attendance and command a premium price. The first of these was deliberately situated near to the city to attract the financial market.

After five years she was 85 per cent booked all year round, with two training centres and a pool of 50 trainers. The business was essentially self-sustaining, gave her a surplus of £10,000 a month, and enabled her to work a very pleasant ten-month year. Amy got there in judicious steps, and she never bragged once.

*1 so your business is under pressure. What now?*

# 2

# *are you disciplined enough to survive?*

make your small business thrive

Lots of people set up their own business only to replicate all the nasty problems that frustrated them in their previous job. If you did this, it's time to reconsider and rip up the straitjackets you built yourself. Have you turned yourself or your company into the very thing you used to hate? It's time to take a new look through the business window, and see what remedies your business needs. Efficiency is a sophisticated form of laziness. The better you are at getting things done, the more time you free up to do what you want. Have you become jaundiced about your business? If so, it is time to take yourself in hand and start afresh. Your business will not survive if your attitude is wrong.

I once met an accountant in Kent. He was a very thoughtful guy, clearly intelligent, and seemingly successful. He had left a larger accountancy practice to set up his own because he felt there was definitely a better way. Excellent. This is the sort of flair and determination that keeps business vital. I then test-drove on him one of my theories about how people approach the administrative aspects of their new businesses, and asked: 'How did you design the administrative systems in your new venture?' The answer held little surprise. 'Oh,' he said, 'we based them on the ones from my previous place.'

This anecdote is not designed to humiliate the man in question, but simply to illustrate one of the oldest pitfalls in the book. That is to say, many people who strike out for a brave new dawn simply end up generating their own version of what they had before, complete with all its flaws and drawbacks. It isn't always the case, but it often is.

## New company: same as the old company?

For those of you who like a bit of rock music, you will be familiar with the line in The Who song *Won't Get Fooled Again*: 'Meet the new boss. Same as the old boss.' You would do well to ask yourself whether this has inadvertently become the case with you personally, or the company you now run. On reflection are you simply replicating the past? Have you invented a genuinely new mousetrap, or is it unnervingly similar to the old one? So here they come again – more nasty questions.

> *'The truth will set you free, but first it will piss you off.'*
>
> Gloria Steinem

* Is your company unnervingly similar to the one you left because you were supposedly fed up with it?
* Have you started behaving similarly to your old boss?
* Did you rather lazily imitate the processes and systems at your previous company when designing your current ones?

**12** make your small business thrive

* Do you have a nagging suspicion that certain things around here do not work particularly well?
* Do you suspect that there is a better way of doing these things?
* Can you think of what they might be?

If the answer to any of these questions is yes, then we have some work to do. It's all about instilling the discipline, both mental and structural, that will free you up to do the rewarding bits more easily and frequently. That's what the question (Are you disciplined enough to survive?) is all about. It means getting rid of any straitjackets that are preventing you or your business from having a decent time of it and being a reasonable success. These straitjackets might be mental, they might be physical, or they might be process-based. Let's have a look at the different types.

## *Ripping up the straitjackets you built yourself*

What's all this about then? Surely, I hear you cry, I haven't built any straitjackets for myself? Well you won't have done it intentionally, but you may have done it nevertheless. What we are referring to here is something that severely limits or restricts you personally, or an aspect of your business. When you think about it, there may be more of them than you would initially like to admit.

> **Straitjacket** (noun): a severe limitation or restriction

Grab a pen and paper, and write these three headings on it, leaving space in the middle to fill out your answers.

1 Mental straitjackets
2 Physical straitjackets
3 Process straitjackets

Have a look at each, and write down your instinctive reaction to what these might be. If none occurs, this could be very good news in that you may well be a highly liberated person, free of constraints, running a business that is brilliantly designed and operates perfectly. How many people do you know in that position? More likely, you have reservations and concerns about all sorts of issues. If the page is blank, or you have already finished with your initial thoughts, then try these prompts.

## Mental straitjackets

* Do I have time to generate new ideas?
* Am I capable of originating new ideas?
* If not, do I know anyone who is that can help?
* Am I able to implement all the ideas I want?

## Physical straitjackets

* Is my working environment appropriate?
* Do I have the right blend of staff or colleagues?
* Do I spend too much time travelling?
* Am I frequently in the wrong place to get things done?

## Process straitjackets

* Do I spend too much time in meetings?
* Do our systems work well?
* Do things get bogged down unnecessarily too often?
* Did I design these systems myself, or were they borrowed from somewhere else?
* Do they genuinely represent the right tools for the job?

If the answers to these questions do not fill you with glee, then chances are it is time to rip up some straitjackets. If that fills you with dread, it shouldn't. Change is good. Trust your instincts. If you know in your heart that something doesn't work very well, and you now have the courage to confess it unwittingly on paper by answering the questions honestly, then it is time for action. Reassure yourself with the knowledge that, whatever it is, it is broken, and it does need fixing. Once you have taken a deep breath and fixed it, you will have far less hassle from that moment on. Of course, this part of the process only forces you to identify the trouble, not cure it. If you are an excellent problem solver, then you may immediately know how to design your own new mousetrap. If not, don't worry, we will work our way through plenty of methods.

> **'Reality is the leading cause of stress among those in touch with it.'**
>
> Lily Tomlin

It takes guts to answer the nasty questions honestly. It takes discipline and determination to do something as a result to improve things. This is your job because you are in charge. Whether that is in charge of 100 people or just yourself doesn't make a jot of difference. It's still down to you. Scary? Perhaps, but it shouldn't be. You are either paid well to do precisely that, or you are doing something because of what you believe in. Either way, it's your job, and the main beneficiary will usually be you. If you take the tough medicine now, you will have a more pleasant time in the future.

We have all heard the maxim *Work to live or live to work?* Which applies to you? Do you work mindlessly because it's there? Or do you use your work as a means to a more fulfilling life? Assuming you would prefer the latter, you need to apply strong discipline to get the business working for you, not the other way round. Let's try another one: *Rule to work or work to rule?* Do you let the strictures of working practices constrain your ability to enjoy working life and flourish in it? Or do you master the situation and make it work for you? The choice is yours. If by any chance it is the former, then I am afraid you may have turned native.

## *Turning native*

What does this mean? It means that you have lost the capability to think independently. It means that you sound and act just like everybody else. The old joke goes like this: when management consultants have been working with their clients for too long, if you look at a video of a meeting between them, with no prior knowledge of who is who, you will not be able to differentiate between the consultants and the clients. Why? Because they are all speaking the same language. Using the same jargon. Wearing the same clothes. The consultants have turned native and are losing their value to their customers. If this is happening to you and your colleagues, change it immediately.

> **'When two people in business always agree, one of them is unnecessary.'**
>
> William Wrigley Junior

It's true isn't it? Under-confident people fail to express their opinion whilst simultaneously failing to recognize that their opinion is precisely what they are paid for. This is true of everybody – staff and consultants. If you don't have a view, what are you there for? So, make sure that you are disciplined enough not to turn native, and that you stay true to your opinions.

> **'An optimist sees an opportunity in every calamity.
> A pessimist sees a calamity in every opportunity.'**
>
> Winston Churchill

So we have spent some time looking at the tethers and straitjackets that constrain your business. You should now be turning your mind to how you can liberate yourself and your business systems to get on and enjoy a better work–life balance. Churchill had a point. What do you see? Glass half empty? Or half full? Or, indeed, do you give a stuff about the supposed glass at all? And what's in the glass, by the way? Methylated spirits or champagne? Life is random, and it is almost impossible to plan. So there will be calamities pretty much every day of the week. But that doesn't mean it's the end of the world, and it doesn't mean you can't generate something positive out of it. So it is your job to engineer an opportunity out of whatever circumstances confront you. That's what this phase is all about: confrontation. That means confronting yourself, and the realities of your business.

# Growing panes: a new look through the business window

Here's a little exercise that might help disentangle the good and bad bits of your working life and your business practices. You've heard of SWOT analysis, and various other systems of analysis such as the Boston Matrix. Well this is the world's simplest one. Take a piece of paper and draw a windowpane on it. On the vertical axis, write GOOD at the top, and BAD at the bottom. On the horizontal axis, write OLD on the left, and NEW on the right. Now take a little time to categorize your habits and techniques. If something you usually do is old and good, then it goes in the top left quadrant, and so on. You will quickly build up a picture of the proportion of good/bad/old/new approaches that you use. Now do the same for those of your business.

If you have several practices in the 'Good and Old' segment, then that is fine. They have obviously stood the test of time, and do the job.

If you have several of them in the 'Good and New' section, even better. This means you are generating new ideas that really work. A blend of old and new is healthy, because it suggests good thinking at the outset, followed by fresh ideas thereafter.

If there is anything in the 'New and Bad' area, it needs careful analysis. It takes guts to reject an idea or process that has only recently been introduced. But surgery here may well be necessary. There may be a case for concluding that the jury is still out so a decision should be given a little more time. But more likely than not, the bad item will remain bad no matter how long you leave it, and the sooner it goes the better. This type of decision can be unpopular, particularly if colleagues have a vested interest, but a bad, ineffective process or idea is just that, and it needs to be eliminated quickly.

Anything in the 'Old and Bad' quadrant is clearly a disaster and has to go immediately.

*'Planning is for the poor.'*

Robert Evans

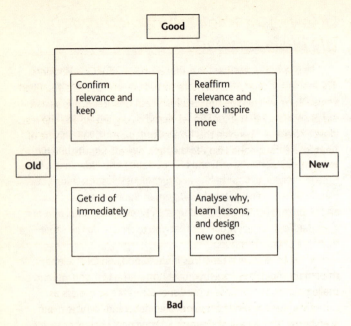

*The growing pane.*

I put the previous quote in to spark a debate. Personally I think it is rubbish. Working out what you want to do and then sorting it out is one of the great fundamentals of having a decent life and a sane mind. You don't have to have endless spreadsheets or spend months over it. Just work out what you want to do, and then do it. The time you dedicate to thinking about things will serve you well when you have to get on and do whatever you have decided. But don't spend too long over it. Trust your instincts. You only have to do three things. It is a fairly straightforward business to write down, but somewhat harder to do. Here they are:

1 Get your head straight
2 Decide what you want to do
3 Do it

# Efficiency is a sophisticated form of laziness

This was an idea that I introduced in *Run Your Own Business*. Think about it carefully. The more sorted you are, the less you need to panic. We will pursue the idea further in Chapter 8. It is such a simple notion. Get the functional elements organized, and the rest slots into place. However, this level of organization will only be of limited use if your head isn't in the right place. Your attitude has to be right too.

# Are you suffering from attitude sickness?

In order to think clearly, you have to have a decent blend of passion and dispassion. If you are horribly biased, you will make poor decisions. Rose-tinted spectacles are as useless as outright cynicism. (For a more detailed debate on cynicism and scepticism, have a look at Chapter 5.) You need a balance, otherwise you will become a danger to yourself. Sounds extreme? Not really. Poor thought leads to unsuccessful management and unsuccessful businesses, and you do not want that state of affairs on your hands. It is all about keeping the mystery alive. In the next chapter, we are going to develop some ways of doing this, but meanwhile, take a moment to reflect on the nasty questions in this chapter and Chapter 1, and consider whether you have genuinely confronted the awkward stuff. Confront the tough issues and ask yourself: Am I disciplined enough to survive? Don't fudge the answer. If you do, you won't get anywhere, and you probably won't survive.

*'Anything can happen in life, especially nothing.'*

Michel Houellebecq

## Flashback

* Are your 'new' approaches the same as your old ones?
* If so, what are you going to do about it?
* Have you identified any mental, physical or process straitjackets?
* If so, what are you going to do about it?
* Have you turned native?
* If so, what are you going to change, and how?
* Have you filled out the Growing Panes grid?
* Have you got rid of any bad things it revealed?
* What have you done about being more organized?
* Is your attitude right?

## Cautionary Tale: Paul Dunn, the impatient Finance Director

Paul was a trained accountant who started in the finance department of a construction company and eventually became the Finance Director. He grew with the company, and after eight years it had become an established top three player in its market.

After enjoying the scale and status for a while, Paul became bored and hankered after doing his own thing. He decided to leave and set up a roving finance service, offering outsourced financial back-up services to companies who either had problems in that area, or who were too small to afford a Finance Director of their own.

The principle seemed reasonable enough – he would start with his construction contacts, and then branch out to advise companies in other markets, because he reckoned his skills were transferable. All fine so far, but when he started working on his own, he missed the status and the support services of his previous company. He simply didn't have the patience to build his business. Instead, he talked in generalities to potential customers, and was found wanting on the delivery. They wanted stuff done, and he was talking broad concepts. Or, to put it another way, they wanted the foundations built and he was describing the penthouse flat.

He probably would have been all right if he had paused at the outset to think carefully about the nature of work that he would pick up in the early days. A quick bit of thought here would have demonstrated that, in all likelihood, his early customers would be small fry. Could he live with that? Would he be happy to muck in until the cash in his new business enabled him to hire someone else to do the grunt work?

If he had been more honest with himself before setting up on his own, he might have realized that he just wasn't cut out for it. Paul was not a success on his own. He soon returned to a conventional Finance Director job in a medium-sized firm, surrounded by all the support services that made him feel good in the first place.

*2 are you disciplined enough to survive?*

# 3

# *thinking is free*

Thinking is free, so do it more often. It is amazing the number of people who do things without knowing why. Remove yourself from the hurly burly of day-to-day life, even for an hour, and think. Too many people pre-judge whether something is going to work or not, particularly if they tried it before and it wasn't a success. Don't fall into this trap. Try things out and if it doesn't work, try something else. The next 'big thing' might be something small. After all, little developments can make a big difference and they are also a lot less scary to embark on. So try lots of little things. Don't overcomplicate what you do or how you explain it to people. Keep it simple, but not simplistic. If something didn't work, then try again. The circumstances may well have changed. Very few 'overnight successes' get it right first time.

*3 thinking is free*

# Thinking is free, so do it more often

**'I haven't had time to think.'**

How many times have we heard that said? Millions of people say it every day in all walks of life, let alone in business. What does it actually mean? If you analyse the phrase carefully, it is complete nonsense. Every sentient being spends the entire day thinking, absorbing circumstances and reacting to them. Of course, the phrase is not literal. What it really means is:

**'I haven't had time to pause and think about the things that really matter, because lots of irrelevant stuff has got in the way.'**

Aha! That's more accurate, and because businesses usually generate vast amounts of irrelevant stuff, businesspeople are very prone to the problem of not having enough thinking time. This is a tragedy, and it is your job to create the appropriate time to rectify the position. Why is this so important? Because, although you may claim that you are too busy to create the time, if you haven't worked out whether what you are doing is the right thing, then you may only be busy pursuing all the wrong things. In a previous book, *Run your own Business*, I asserted that you should never do anything unless you know why you are doing it. This sounds blindingly obvious, and yet people frequently do.

So now is the time to get thinking. It is a free activity. All you have to do is set aside the time and create the appropriate conditions. Some people like total peace and seclusion, others like something to shake them up. Work out your style by answering these questions to help you develop different ways of creating thinking time.

Are you likely to have some decent ideas if you:
* sit on top of a mountain
* have a massage
* get on the running machine

* visit an art gallery
* disappear to a country cottage
* drink a bottle of quality wine
* go for a bike ride
* leave the country for the day
* take a ride in a hot air balloon
* visit the zoo
* go fishing?

You get the idea. The activity or circumstance doesn't matter, so long as it is different from where you normally are, and what you normally do.

> *'A great many people think they are thinking, when they are merely rearranging their prejudices.'*
>
> William James

If everything is too samey, or things aren't going that well, it's time for a re-think. And that does not mean rearranging your prejudices, or dreaming up new reasons to prove that you are right about something. It means taking a hard look at what you've got and working out whether it is any good or not, and whether you like your circumstances. If you have any doubts about any aspect of your life or business, it has to be done. Even in the unlikely event that you don't have any concerns at all about anything, it is still a great thing to do. Everything can always be made better or more stimulating.

## Try this. It might just work

You have to enter the thinking process in the right frame of mind. It's no use being petrified, depressed, cynical, paranoid, resentful, jaded or any other negative emotion. It is okay to be a bit vexed or concerned. It is all right to be mildly sceptical. It is fine to be quizzical. In fact, that should positively be encouraged. Your objective should be to let a little light in on your circumstances and view it as though you were someone else looking at you. Strange,

**3 *thinking is free***

and quite detaching, but ultimately rewarding. Start with some general questions:

* How well is the business doing?
* What are the prospects for survival?
* Do you want evolution or revolution?
* Are you facing hard or soft decisions?
* Are you planning the 'next big thing'?

Be positive. You have to believe, 'If I try this, it might just work.'

## Why the next big thing might be small

A lot of people get hung up on planning the 'next big thing'. But who is to say that the next big thing has to be big? Sometimes tiny increments of change make amazing things happen. If you are unconvinced of this, read Malcolm Gladwell's book, *The Tipping Point*. It demonstrates how little things can make a big difference, if cunningly applied. So don't panic about the fear that you need to come up with something outstandingly original. People rarely do. Occasionally someone like Edison will invent a light bulb, but that's a bit beyond our remit here. If by any chance you are a genius, then put this book down immediately – there's nothing I can teach you.

**'God is in the details.'**

Anonymous artist

There has been a huge amount of hoo-ha about 'the big idea'. Nothing wrong with that, but when you run a business, there is also great mileage to be had from lots of little ideas. Little ideas are great. They are less hard to come up with, they are usually cheaper and easier to implement, and they can be done more quickly. This enables you to work out rapidly whether they are any good or not. No one wants to admit that a big idea is rubbish once it has been implemented, so they are hard to rectify even if everybody can see that they aren't working very well. An example of this would be when Coca-Cola replaced their original version with a new one. Eventually they had to reissue it as Coke Classic. They got it right in the end, but it took a while for anyone to admit that the new 'big idea'

**26** make your small business thrive

wasn't working. In comparison, little ideas can be test-driven constantly, refined, enlarged, developed or withdrawn with the minimum of fuss. Try making your next big thing small. You might surprise yourself.

## A strategy is when you have decided what to do

Complicated thinking is another cul-de-sac. Do not fall into the trap of thinking that an idea needs to be complicated, or that your route to it needs to be either. Good ideas are usually simple, as is the means by which they are conceived. Most people have heard of the KISS acronym, Keep It Simple Stupid. Whilst I admire the sentiment behind it, I am not a fan of the Stupid bit. You are not stupid, nor are most people who run businesses. So I have taken the double liberty of both adapting KISS, and inventing a new one: KITSCH. Here they are.

## KISS: Keep It Simple and Sensible

It's the sensible bit that makes the difference for me. You're not daft, and you instinctively know what is likely to work. So keep it sensible as well as simple. This acronym may or may not be memorable because it has the same letters as the old one. So here is a new version that makes it clearer. It is longer and, of course, it presupposes that you can remember how to spell KITSCH, but it makes the point. In this one, the Sensible element is represented by the words Cool Headed, and the simplicity part is additionally emphasized by the adjective Terribly.

## KITSCH: Keep It Terribly Simple and Cool Headed

The *Terribly* element here forces you to be ruthless about the simplicity of the idea. If you can't express it in one or two

*3 thinking is free* **27**

sentences, it is probably too complicated. If your mate who doesn't know your industry can understand it, it is probably all right. It doesn't mean it is any good, but at least it's clear. Then comes the cool-headed part. There is no point in generating a head of steam about a new idea until you have worked it through properly. Passion is good. Enthusiasm is as well. But not if either are misdirected. If you let your heart run away with an idea before you have worked it out properly, you will waste your time and possibly your money.

> **'You do not really understand something unless you can explain it to your grandmother.'**
>
> Albert Einstein

This approach is simple, but not simplistic. It means you are not allowed to wrap yourself up in incomprehensible words. No impenetrable jargon! No spreadsheets! Just a pen and plenty of paper, your preferred thinking conditions, and an appropriate chunk of time dedicated to the matter in hand. If you need a little help and stimulation to increase the chances of your having some decent ideas, there are hundreds of books dedicated to the subject. One of the best is *Flicking your Creative Switch* by Wayne Lotherington.

Here are some other enigmatic thoughts to help you along:
* Stand back and take a closer look
* Death to compromise
* Look before you reap
* Other people's thoughts can't kill you, but your own could
* Other people's thoughts can't kill you, but your own could keep you alive
* Start with a bang, then bang again
* Watch for shapes, then nip into the gaps
* Ski off-piste for once
* When the others zig, zag. Then zog.

One thing is for sure: it takes time and concentration, so don't think you can get away with a quick fix or a cursory skim over the issues. Muster all your mental energy and create the right conditions to allow your thoughts to flow properly.

> *'If a problem is hard, think, think, then think again. It will hurt at first, but you'll get used to it.'*
>
> Barbara Castle

## Didn't work? Try again

In his book *Outliers*, Malcolm Gladwell explains that Easterners have a stronger work ethic and so are better at maths because they are used to taking a lot of time to solve problems. This is the kind of tenacious attitude that you need to adopt when you are ensuring the survival of your business. If one piece of thinking or initiative doesn't work, then try another. And another. You are effectively testing each hypothesis in turn, like a good scientist, in an iterative process that allows you to learn as you go along. If you stop too early, you'll never know. As *Private Eye* notes:

> *'The scientific method consists of a researcher putting forward a new proposal and his or her colleagues testing the living daylights out of it without fear of the consequences.'*

This takes tenacity, persistence, and an unswerving resolve that you will eventually get a result. So when you feel like stopping, keep going.

> *'The mark of an educated mind is to be able to entertain an idea without accepting it.'*
>
> Aristotle

You have now pretty much completed your preparation for quality thinking. Be open-minded about what you come up with. Remember the Sensible element of the revised KISS principle. Adopt the attitude that 'If I try this, it might just work'. Consider the small stuff as well as the large, and steer clear of supposed big ideas and flabby management concepts that could distract you from the relevance of a clear, simple idea.

*3 thinking is free*

## Flashback

* Have you created the time to think?
* If so, when exactly, and for how long?
* Where are you going to do your thinking?
* How is this environment different from your normal one?
* Have you consulted any relevant books?
* Have you examined and dismissed distracting management concepts?
* Are you prepared to be open-minded?
* Are you ready to consider small things as well as large?
* How are you going to keep it simple?
* Are you genuinely prepared to try out the ideas you generate?

## Success Story: Mike Simmons, the market researcher who emulated the big boys from the beginning

Setting the right tone is always difficult when running a company. Sometimes it is called culture. Sometimes style. Whatever you call it, it all starts at the beginning, and it starts at the top.

Mike worked for a large market research company, and after a few years he concluded that the company's culture just wasn't his style. After a lot of thought, he did two things – he decided to leave, and he spent a long time working out what style of company he would like to set up.

This process was not borne out of arrogance. Mike knew in his heart that there is simply no point in working for a company if you don't really fit in with their way of doing things. So he wrote down the sort of company he would be proud of working for, and set about creating it. The business plan and, crucially, the recruitment policy, directly enacted his closely held beliefs.

Part of this belief was not to kowtow to larger firms. He couldn't stand it. He insisted that all his people could hold their own with the big boys. Again, this was not to manifest itself in arrogance, simply in the kind of intellectual quality and operational integrity that you would expect from the best in any field of business.

His staff loved it, because it imbued them with a much higher level of respect than they had experienced in their former jobs. His people were trusted and given a lot of rope. As a result, they behaved highly responsibly with clients, and enjoyed the sort of autonomy that suggests quality. That, of course, meant they could charge more as a company, and all enjoy top salaries.

This happy state of affairs all stemmed from Mike's broadmindedness at the outset. He set the style, and success followed.

*3 thinking is free*

# 4

# *thinking stage 1: what are the facts?*

Rivers and dams are a simple enough analogy to work out what's good and bad in your business. What flows well and what causes blockages? Introduce more rivers and unblock the dams as fast as possible. If you are stuck in a rut, then make sure you use purely factual, near scientific ways of looking at your business. Don't let opinion come into it until you have the correct information. If something seems nuts in your business, then apply a healthy dose of common sense. When looking back at successes in your business to search for inspiration, always admit if something was a fluke. Far too many people rewrite history to claim that a random success was carefully thought through. Don't fool yourself. If things are drifting, take the time to remind yourself of the original point of your business.

The first step of the process is based solely on the facts. At this point we are not interested in your opinion, or those of others. This is not because they are not valid or useful, but because they place an angle on the facts that will hinder us at first. So we are going to get the truth out on the table and examine it. This is what a client of mine used to call 'having the drains up'. If you find yourself fudging the answers, rip them up and start again. We do not want our thinking to suffer from factual pollution.

## Rivers and dams

First of all, imagine your business as a series of rivers and dams. These will be areas where everything is flowing well, or where there are frequently blockages that prevent you from conducting your business properly. Before you start, consider whether this process should be conducted on your own, or in the presence of others. If you are self-employed, or in charge of a company whose every workings are well known to you, then it might be a solo project. If not, it might be a suitable methodology for a brainstorm or awayday. The latter will be appropriate if you are unaware of all the facts yourself. After you have read how the process works, revisit this point because once you have seen all the questions you will have a clearer idea of whether you are fully qualified to answer them all or not. The first step is to ask some questions and write down the answers.

Remember that rivers are things that flow well, and dams are places where they do not. We will start with the good stuff.

* Where are the rivers?
* How many of them are there?
* How large?
* How small?
* How many in total?

Put that to one side for a minute and take a deep breath. We are moving on to the not-so-good things.

* Where are the dams?
* How many of them are there?

* How large?
* How small?
* How many in total?

And put that list on the side. If it was a harrowing exercise, go for a walk or pour a stiff drink. Now answer the next question.

* Which do you have more of – rivers or dams?

This basic exercise should allow you to see at a glance what works in your business, and what doesn't. It will also reveal straightaway whether the business has more good things going on than bad, or vice versa. Don't panic at this stage if there seem to be way more dams than rivers. That's what we are here to sort out.

## Send it down to the boys in forensic or go completely ballistic?

The next step is examining the truth. I used to work with a guy who, whenever we received a written request from a client, would say: 'Send it down to the boys in forensic.' The gist of it was that we needed the full rundown on the subject matter and the task in hand before we could start pontificating about any possible solutions. He was right. These days, they call it strategic planning. Whatever you call it, it needs to be a great inquisition of all the available information. To get to the heart of the matter, it is worth looking at the definitions of 'forensic' and 'forensics'.

---

**Forensic** (adjective): relating to, or used in, a court of law

---

'Forensic' as an adjective means relating to, or used in a court of law. That means whatever it refers to must be solely concerned with the facts. Strangely though, the noun 'forensics' refers to the study of formal debating, which is an opinion-based and non-factual pursuit.

---

**Forensics** (noun): the art or study of formal debating

---

*4  thinking stage 1: what are the facts?*                    **35**

So we are going to deploy a different, more scientific term to define this stage of our factual line of enquiry. The inspiration comes from the world of ballistics. Ballistics is only concerned with the facts, and at this stage, so are we. We are going to concentrate on the structural elements of your business, the tangible ones. Using the language of ballistics, we will divide the business into manageable chunks that we can then analyse.

> **Ballistics** (noun): the study of the flight dynamics of projectiles; the interaction of the forces of propulsion, projectile aerodynamics, atmospheric resistance and gravity

Get out another clean sheet of paper and split it into five sections, each with a heading: projectiles, propulsion forces, aerodynamics, resistance and gravity. This is what the headings refer to:

* **Projectiles:** who, or what, is heading where?
* **Propulsion forces:** who, or what, is making them do that?
* **Aerodynamics:** who, or what, has good momentum behind it?
* **Resistance:** who, or what, is resisting forward motion?
* **Gravity:** is there anything structural that anchors any of this?

Don't fill the headings in at this stage. Put the piece of paper to one side. You might need it in a minute.

*'Men occasionally stumble over the truth, but most of them pick themselves up and hurry off as if nothing happened.'*

Winston Churchill

## Common sense analysis

Now it is time to analyse what you've got. Stick to the facts and nothing else at this stage. We want the truth and nothing but.

**36**   make your small business thrive

Don't ignore it. If you do, it will still be there tomorrow. Use your common sense. Common Sense Analysis is something I originally developed at university with my tutorial partner, Nick Middleton. There is no technique, other than using common sense – the sort that you would expect from a layperson in a pub. If there is a technique, it lies in the brutal simplicity of the questions, and the production of jargon-free answers. By now you should have roughly three piles of paper – one of rivers, one of dams, and one of ballistics. I say piles because you may be running a large, complicated business. If there is a lot of material, you might want to take a while to sort the wheat from the chaff and organize it into easily discernible parts.

Put the 'river' information on the table and stare at it. Ask yourself this question:

* Why do these bits work so well?

Do not rush the answer(s). Write them down. Now apply some common sense analysis with more questions.

* Is that really the reason?
* Could it be for other reasons?
* If that is the reason, can I take it and apply it somewhere else in the business?
* Can I think of other possible applications?

From this process, you should be able to generate a highly promising list of ideas that emulate good things that your business already does. In other words, if something is a success, work out why and replicate it elsewhere. Some words of caution here though: always admit if something was a fluke.

Under no circumstances should you come away from this piece of analysis concluding that you should replicate something good elsewhere when you don't actually know why it worked in the first place. Sometimes, things just work through luck. Combinations of factors collide – timing, pricing, packaging, outside factors – to make something work, whether you planned them that way or not. If you were genuinely surprised by the success of something, and are not sure of the reasons behind that success, then admit it.

*4  thinking stage 1: what are the facts?*

Do not go around pretending that you planned it all along – it will come back to bite you at some point. Just use the good thing to stimulate the next good thing. Use the principle: so that worked – have I got any more good ideas based on that?

Now put the 'dams' on the table. This bit may be less pleasant, but it will be just as instructive. Ask yourself the question:

* Why do these bits not work well?

Write down the answers and again apply common sense analysis by probing with more questions.

* Is that really the reason?
* Could it be for other reasons?
* If so, what are they?
* If that is the reason, how can I fix it?
* If I can't fix it, who can?

If you can't see a clear way through it all, don't panic. Grab your ballistics sheet and review the headings.

* **Projectiles:** who, or what, is heading where?
* **Propulsion forces:** who, or what, is making them do that?
* **Aerodynamics:** who, or what, has good momentum behind it?
* **Resistance:** who, or what, is resisting forward motion?
* **Gravity:** is there anything structural that anchors any of this?

Now reorganize the rivers and dams information by the ballistics categories. Use the questions associated with each component to try to unravel how something might be resolved. For example, does a resistance question help solve an issue? Does the gravity of the business explain why something is as it is? Does a propulsion force provide a clue as to how to fix a dam? Here is a full set of examples.

### Projectiles

* Are we dealing with a projectile here?
* Who, or what, is heading where?
* Is that good or bad?

**38**  make your small business thrive

* If it's good, how can it be replicated elsewhere?
* If it's bad, how can it be fixed?

## Propulsion forces
* Are we dealing with a propulsion force?
* Who, or what, is making them do that?
* Is that good or bad?
* If it's good, how can it be replicated elsewhere?
* If it's bad, how can it be fixed?

## Aerodynamics
* Is this to do with aerodynamics?
* Who, or what, has good momentum behind it?
* How can that be harnessed?

## Resistance
* Is this a case of resistance?
* Who, or what, is resisting forward motion?
* How can that be fixed?

## Gravity
* Is gravity at work here?
* Is there something structural or cultural anchoring this?
* Can that be turned to our advantage or does it need fixing?

*'When the facts change, I change my mind. What do you do?'*

John Maynard Keynes

Hopefully, this type of cross-examination should be helping to shed any fuzzy thinking. Remember we are still only dealing in the realms of fact. It is your job to face the facts maturely, and see them for what they are. Do not let bias and prejudice creep in to your thinking, and be prepared to change your mind if the facts suggest that it would be a good idea to do so.

*'The more you learn the worse things get.'*

Mark Twain

*4  thinking stage 1: what are the facts?*　　**39**

There may be a certain element here of not wanting to face the truth, but you must. Take heart from the fact that all intelligent people and successful businesses learn from mistakes. This is the very essence of all successful evolution. If you are not capable of working out what went wrong and how it could be done better next time, then your business will never evolve. So be reassured that making mistakes is perfectly fine, so long as you are able to identify them accurately, and then take the necessary remedial action.

*'Mistakes are the portals of discovery.'*

James Joyce

It was once said that we all make mistakes, and when we have made enough, they call it experience. Do not be afraid of mistakes. They usually lead to something else, particularly if they are absorbed humbly and thoughtfully. Another way of looking at it is that you can't make any mistakes if you don't do anything, and vice versa. If you never cook, you never spill any ingredients on the floor. If you never wash up, you never break any plates. Some form of action with a few flaws is far preferable to inaction.

*'The man who makes no mistakes does not usually make anything.'*

Edward John Phelps

*'I've learnt from my mistakes, and I'm sure I can repeat them.'*

Peter Cook

Also be aware that you need to approach your thinking with the right tools for the job. If an issue is highly technical, then you may wish to use this process alongside someone who knows the technical detail, and can therefore answer the majority of the tricky questions that it throws up. There's no point in generating scores of questions that you cannot personally answer, unless it is your specific intent to raise them all, and then go to the experts for their solutions. Far better to embark on the process with an approximate idea of what you think might emerge, and have the necessary people on hand to help you out.

**Rivers**
- Where are the rivers?
- How many of them are there?
- How large?
- How small?
- How many in total?

**Dams**
- Where are the dams?
- How many of them are there?
- How large?
- How small?
- How many in total?

**Ballistics**

**Projectiles:** who, or what, is heading where?
**Propulsion forces:** who, or what, is making them do that?
**Aerodynamics:** who, or what, has good momentum behind it?
**Resistance:** who, or what, is resisting forward motion?
**Gravity:** is there anything structural that anchors any of this?

**Common Sense Analysis**

**Rivers**
- Why do these bits work so well?
- Is that *really* the reason?
- Could it be for other reasons?
- If that is the reason, can I take it and apply it somewhere else in the business?
- If so, can I write a list of other possible applications of this finding?

**Dams**
- Why do these bits not work well?
- Is that *really* the reason?
- Could it be for other reasons?
- If so, what are they?
- If that is the reason, how can I fix it?
- If I can't fix it, who can?

*Thinking stage 1: Facts.*

> **'If all you have is a hammer, everything begins to look like a nail.'**
>
> Nietzsche

4 thinking stage 1: what are the facts?

Diving in to any wide-ranging thought process without decent preparation is inadvisable. If you embark on it with only one angle, you may only generate the one solution, and it will probably be the same as everything you have come up with before. Most issues have multiple possible solutions, so you need to stay open-minded as to what these might be. This may mean that, if you adopt this thinking technique, you might want to run it in parallel with another method to see if you emerge with a richer combination of ideas and answers.

> **'When you have a hammer all problems start to look like a nail. But when you don't have a hammer, you don't want anything to look like a nail.'**
>
> Robert Kagan

I guess Nietzsche made his observation long before Robert Kagan, but his addition to the analogy makes an interesting point. If you embark on some careful thought without any techniques or any shape to organize your thinking, then you may well only emerge with a re-statement of your problems. So try to regard this technique as your hammer, and hit those nails right on the head.

## Always admit if something was a fluke

A quick word of warning about the positive things that fall into the rivers category. Do not be tempted to claim that these things were wonderfully devised and thought through if, in truth, they were actually a fluke. Only you know the reality of this. If you allow this fuzzy thinking to happen, then you will assume that their success will be replicated if you repeat them, but you will simply be throwing your business open to random forces of chance. So don't do it. Have the maturity to accept that it was a fluke, and don't build your next move on a fallacy of the past.

## Remind me, what was the original idea?

One final point on the Facts stage: if you find yourself getting in a muddle, do stop and ask yourself this fundamental question: What *was* the original idea? It could refer to anything — why you set the business up in the first place, what the vision or purpose of your company is, why you bother to come to work in the morning — anything that is crucial to the matter in hand. The original idea always lies at the heart of what is important. So remind yourself what it was in the first place, and use that as an anchor point to prevent your thoughts from drifting off into weird areas that don't help you on to the next thing.

## *Flashback*

* Have you written out your lists of rivers and dams?
* Did you analyse them carefully to find out why things are as they are?
* What did you conclude?
* Did you try the ballistic questions?
* What did that reveal?
* Did you look at your successes to see if they were flukes?
* Have you worked out how to replicate good things elsewhere?
* Have you revisited your original idea for the business?
* How are you going to fix the bad bits?
* What was the mistake you learnt most from and why?

# 5

# *thinking stage 2: what's your own opinion?*

It always seems odd when your doctor tells you that smoking will kill you when he smokes himself. Don't be that doctor! Apply all your experience to your business and practice what you preach. Ask yourself what the most sensible view on your business is, and apply that straightaway. You need to be able to come to a balanced view about your business. The sceptic asks if an idea is truly feasible. The cynic says it will never work. And the pragmatist works out whether it is worth it and how it can be done. Once you have thought about something carefully and decided to do it, do it properly, and don't cut corners. Trust your own instinct. It will be accurate and helpful about 80% of the time. So if it feels right, then do it. You can always change your mind later.

*5  thinking stage 2: what's your own opinion?*

# The doctor who died of ill health

So you have the facts on the table in front of you. What works, and what doesn't. Now is the time to introduce your opinion to the equation. You will be familiar with the phrase 'heed your own counsel'. And yet life is full of examples of people who fail to do precisely that. Whether it is true or not, received wisdom suggests that doctors always tell you how to live longer, that smoking is bad, and that you need to improve your fitness and your diet. But do they practise what they preach? Frequently not. Decorators often have tatty houses that need a lick of paint. They don't want to come home and do for themselves what they do all day for a living. And advertising agencies are often poor at promoting themselves, despite the fact that they do it successfully every day for their clients.

So the point is, you give out good advice all day – are you capable of paying attention to your own advice? This is what this section is all about: heeding your own counsel, and listening to your own opinion.

---

**Opinion** (noun): judgement or belief not founded on certainty or proof

---

The facts will, in the main, speak for themselves, and the nasty home truths certainly will, so don't dwell on those. Now start considering what your perspective on the issues is. If you are conducting this process as part of a strategic rethink with colleagues, then you might want to get them to contribute their opinions too. Just make sure that people don't all dive in with their opinions and prejudices at the beginning. Make sure that stage 1 (in Chapter 4) has been done first. Then you can evaluate their opinions in the context of the facts, rather than just as a random series of views.

> *'Don't argue for the difficulties. The difficulties will argue for themselves.'*
>
> Winston Churchill

**46** make your small business thrive

You should always trust your instincts. Up until the mid-1980s, it was normal for people in business to have a hunch and go with it. Then came research, pre-testing, and a range of other techniques for checking if an idea was viable before it ever saw the light of day. For enormous product launches that require multi-million pound investments, that is totally valid. But for simple, ingenious ways of galvanizing your business, it is totally unnecessary. Have a hunch and go for it. If it doesn't work, do something else. It's that simple. In Chapter 3, we talked about how the next big thing might be small, and I referred to Malcolm Gladwell's book, *The Tipping Point*. Well, he has since written another book called *Blink*. The central tenet of it is that a snap judgement made very quickly can actually be more effective than one made deliberately and cautiously. He introduces the notion of thin slicing, in which the impression gained of something in the first two seconds is almost always more reliable than one built up over a longer period of time.

So trust your instincts, and those of respected colleagues. Do not ignore your own counsel and become a doctor who dies of ill health, having failed to listen to your own advice. We will start by dragging your opinions out of you, and then go on to introduce some devil's advocate elements to test-drive those opinions for validity.

## *Heed your own counsel*

Take your sheets of rivers, dams and ballistics, and re-read them. Work through each in turn, asking yourself these questions. Remember to heed your own counsel.

* What do I personally think of this issue?
* What does my colleague think?
* If it's a bad thing, do I know how to fix it?
* If it's a good thing, how can I develop it?
* What is my immediate thought about what to do next?

Write down the answers to these and put them on one side. Now start making some decisions. If an idea is rubbish, throw it away. By now, some of the ideas will have bitten the dust, and those

*5  thinking stage 2: what's your own opinion?*          **47**

that remain on the table are probably pretty robust. Review what is left and, if necessary, write them out again because they may have taken a bit of a battering on the way. It is worthwhile taking the time to do this because scribbled ideas with too many comments on them are often confusing. Ideally, an idea should consist of one word or one sentence. If expressed that simply, it is much easier to determine whether it is going to work or not. Only ever put one idea on one piece of paper, so as not to confuse or interlink any of them. Chuck away all the old scribbles and go off and do something different. If you have been at it for a while, take a breather or come back to it tomorrow. So, to recap, you should now have just one pile of paper, each with one idea on it, expressed either as one sentence or, better still, one word.

## The pragmatist who was sceptical about the cynic

Now we are going to introduce the devil's advocate, or the devil's avocado as an old colleague always used to say. As you know, that is an opposing, and often unpopular, view and in business these can take various forms. For this part of the thinking process, I have chosen two views: sceptical and cynical. Once we have examined these in detail, we will counterbalance them with a healthy dose of pragmatism.

Let's start at the sharp end. A cynic is someone who thinks the worst of almost every person or situation. At their most extreme, they are no fun to have around. Sometimes they are called killers, because they only ever kill ideas and they never seem to have any themselves.

---

**Cynic** (noun): a person who believes the worst about people or the outcome of events

---

As a personality trait, therefore, cynicism is not very desirable, but as an aid to rational thought, it can be very helpful in sorting

**48**   make your small business thrive

out which ideas are good and which are lousy. Hundreds of years ago, a cynic was a member of a sect founded by a guy called Antisthenes. These people scorned worldly things and believed that self-control was the key to the only good available in the world. A pretty heavy notion I'm sure you'll agree, but that's by the by. For our purposes, a short, sharp blast of cynicism will sort the wheat from the chaff, the good ideas from the not-so-good. As the saying goes, 'The good is the enemy of the great'. In fact, some people are active fans of cynicism, and believe it is as close as you can get to truly accurate observation.

> *'The power of accurate observation is often called cynicism by those who do not have it.'*
>
> George Bernard Shaw

So we are going to cross-examine our ideas with a set of cynical questions. You might think that this approach is a bit strange, but there is a method behind the madness. You have probably come across Edward de Bono's system of putting on different coloured hats to represent different character types and ways of thinking. Well, this is similar, but you can do it on your own. It forces you to adopt frames of mind that you wouldn't usually consider if left to your own devices and, crucially, it enables you to replicate the possible reactions of colleagues and customers to the new ideas. So the next part of this stage is to ask a series of cynical questions. Here we go.

* What's the point of that?
* That will never work, will it?
* That didn't work before so it won't work now, will it?
* They'll never go for that, will they?
* How can we afford that?
* No one is going to buy that, are they?

I haven't gone on and on with a long list, because the negative nature of these questions is quite draining. Don't overdo it, just briefly adopt the position of someone who cannot see a way through for the proposed idea. It will rapidly reveal whether the initiative can withstand aggressive scrutiny.

*5 thinking stage 2: what's your own opinion?* **49**

Now we are going to move on to a milder line of enquiry, basing it on scepticism.

Originally a sceptic was a member of one of the ancient Greek schools of philosophy, populated by people like Pyrrho, who believed that real knowledge of things is impossible. Another rather weighty philosophical thought, but again, not one that should put us off much. Sceptics aren't saying no to something, they just aren't convinced. What they want is more proof that something is likely to work. There is a lovely moment in a book called *The Pirate Inside* by Adam Morgan where he describes the personal characteristics that make individuals in companies agitate for change. When interviewing Bob Gill of Pringles, he asks him what his reaction is whenever someone says no to an idea. 'Oh,' he says, 'you basically treat the word no as a request for further information.' How brilliant is that? Ever the optimist, lively bright people in business believe so much in their ideas that they just keep going until everybody else says yes. So consider this sceptical element of the evolutive thinking process as a request for further verification that the idea in question does indeed have merit.

Go back to your pile of ideas, and subject them to some further interrogation.

---

**Sceptical** (adjective): not convinced that something is true; tending to mistrust people and ideas

---

* How will that work then?
* Will it be viable?
* Will people be impressed by it?
* Will it complement the current business well?
* Can the idea be pushed even further?
* Are there even more possibilities beyond that?

It doesn't matter in what order you ask these questions, nor whether you ask the cynical set before or after this sceptical set. The important thing is that you have embarked on some form of

**50**　make your small business thrive

elimination process. This will ensure that you don't waste time later pursuing ideas when you could already have worked out for yourself that they probably wouldn't work anyway.

> *'If one regards oneself as a sceptic, it is as well from time to time to be sceptical about one's scepticism.'*
>
> Freud

Round three takes the pragmatist's perspective. This is where we survey the two extreme sets of opinions and draw them together to strike some sort of sensible balance. This is not the same as killing a perfectly good idea. It is sense-checking the likelihood of something actually getting done.

> **Pragmatism** (noun): the doctrine that the content of a concept consists only in its practical applicability

An idea is only as good as your ability to enact it, so what we now need is a pragmatic check. Review the ideas asking these questions.
* Can you afford it?
* Have you got the resources to implement it?
* Will customers and colleagues accept it?
* Have you got the time to do it?

For more than 200 questions on whether something can truly be done, read *So What?*

# Death to compromise

You should be down to a highly manageable number by now, so all that is left is a reality check and some fine-tuning. Pause for a minute or, as a colleague of mine used to say, stand back and take a closer look. This is the point at which you need to agree if you are happy to go public with the ideas. There is no room for compromise here. You are either going to do it, or you are not.

*5 thinking stage 2: what's your own opinion?*

* Is there any element of bluff or self-delusion in it?
* Is it a forced fit or does it sit comfortably with everything else?
* Could it be better articulated?
* Is it free of jargon?
* Can you relate to it?
* Will other people?
* Are you happy to go public with it?

---

**Compromise** (noun): settlement by concessions on both sides; something midway between two or more different things

---

That's pretty much it. Just don't compromise the idea or how you are going to execute it. Remember: you are either going to do it, or you are not. Be decisive, and get ready to enact it.

> *'Consensus is when we have a discussion. They tell me what they think. Then I decide.'*
>
> Lee Iacocca

This chapter was all about coming to decisions. You have covered a lot of ground now, so it is time to pause and reflect. You should have taken the facts, and overlaid your own opinion. If that was a bit wishy-washy in places, the cynical or sceptical view should have helped to crystallize your opinion, so that you could reach a consensus with yourself. You should have ended up with one clear pile of ideas, rigorously sense-checked for their practicability. In a way, therefore, you are ready to enact them, and if you feel completely confident in them, then do go ahead and do that now. If you are still anxious, discuss them with a colleague.

### Heed your own counsel

- What do I personally think of this issue?
- What does my colleague think?
- If it's a bad thing, do I know how to fix it?
- If it's a good thing, how can I develop it?
- What is my immediate thought about what to do next?

### Sceptical view

- How will that work then?
- Will it be viable?
- Will people be impressed by it?
- Will it complement the current business well?
- Can the idea be pushed even further?
- Are there even more possibilities beyond that?

### Cynical view

- What's the point of that?
- That will never work, will it?
- That didn't work before so it won't work now, will it?
- They'll never go for that, will they?
- How can we afford that?
- No one is going to buy that, are they?

### Pragmatic check

- Can you afford it?
- Have you got the resources to implement it?
- Will customers and colleagues accept it?
- Have you got the time to do it?

### Compromise check

- Is there any element of bluff or self-delusion in it?
- Is it a forced fit or does it sit comfortably with everything else?
- Could it be better articulated?
- Is it free of jargon?
- Can you relate to it?
- Will other people?
- Are you happy to go public with it?

*Thinking stage 2: Own opinion.*

5  thinking stage 2: what's your own opinion?

## Flashback

* Have you heeded your own counsel?
* Have you trusted your instincts?
* Did you adopt the cynical position?
* Did that force you to reject some ideas?
* Did you pose the sceptical questions?
* Have you overcome those reservations or clarified things as a result?
* What did the pragmatic check reveal?
* Have you compromised at all in any of this?
* Are you ready to go public with the ideas?
* Have you paused to reflect on progress so far?

## Success Story: Gordon Allman, the television producer who realized that the 'next big thing' could be small

Success is relative. Growth may or may not matter. It depends what you want from life, and how much you feel the need to tell anyone who will listen how wonderfully successful you are, and how fast your supposedly amazing business is growing.

Gordon began life as a television producer in a top ten advertising agency in their heyday in the 1980s and 1990s, enjoying top pay and budgets that often stretched to millions of pounds. Technology and a couple of recessions changed all that. Fast forward 20 years and clients would expect to pay £30,000 for a commercial rather than ten times the amount, and technology made it happen much faster, often missing out layers of human expertise.

Many high-ranking producers left the industry, retired to Spain or retreated to Devon to write their long-promised novel. Not Gordon. He was convinced that there was still mileage in the tank, and didn't see any reason why he shouldn't be able to apply his experience to the industry even though budgets had shrunk and the technology had moved on.

He investigated all the permutations thoroughly. Researching the new technology was not difficult – it just took an inquisitive mind and some proper thinking time. Designing a business model that would work on the reduced budgets was more of a challenge, but it definitely could be done. He calculated that he could have a decent life by doing two jobs a month, with an average budget of £30,000 and a margin of 20 per cent, so that's how he started, positioning himself as 'big company experience in a small package' (he wasn't that tall, which helped with the banter too).

Gordon was a success because he was able to adapt to changing market conditions. He subsumed his ego and got on with designing the next thing. Once he had established his proposition and cut his cloth accordingly, he was able to build a thriving business, always working on the principle that the next big thing might be small.

*5 thinking stage 2: what's your own opinion?*

# 6
# *set up your business tripwires and grenades*

56  make your small business thrive

If you know you are not very good at something, or are likely to forget to do it, then do something now to anticipate that difficulty and thus increase your effectiveness when the time comes. Design your tripwires now to improve all aspects of your business. Explosive ideas have the power to turbo-charge your business but they don't occur all by themselves. You need to engineer time and space to invent clever interventions that will ignite your business. If you can't cope with doing everything at once, then consider doing things in a sequence. Even one in a row is good. Do simple tasks first and fast, and liberate proper time for more complex tasks. Only put the effort in where it gets you somewhere. Think carefully before you rush into something.

## How to trip yourself up on purpose

So you have done a lot of thinking, and now is the time to decide how precisely you are going to implement the great ideas you have generated. We don't want them languishing on a piece of paper in a drawer somewhere and never seeing the light of day. Getting them done will require a mixture of business effort and personal effort, and in this chapter we are going to deal with the business perspective. It is all about setting up your business tripwires so that you cannot fail to action something. Many of us know that if we don't write something down, we will most likely forget it. That could be a sticky note on the back of the door saying 'don't forget keys', a shopping list, or a note on the steering wheel saying 'oil' or 'petrol'. Whatever the task, if you write it down and put it in the right place, it becomes impossible to forget the important thing when the time comes. This is the principle behind business tripwires. We are going to work out what will go wrong *before* it does, and put the measures in place to prevent that from happening. To make this really effective, you need to have the drains up and work out how everything works, and work out where it is most likely to fall down. Predict that, and you will ensure that the important things truly get done.

> **'If you're going to do something, go start. Life's simpler than we sometimes can admit.'**
>
> Robert De Niro

## Write it down and it gets done

Discussing broad concepts in their embryonic phase can be fun, particularly for those who don't have to get the thing in question done. But nothing irritates a decent business person more than a good idea that hasn't quite seen the light of day. No one cares why – the point is, it is still on the drawing board and the fruits of it have not been realized. Often this is because there is confusion about whose responsibility it actually is. Other times it is because the idea is allowed to drift and no one pushes for any particular deadline to be met. The trick is to write it down. As Robert De Niro says, if you intend to start, then start. It's that simple. The precise list of what needs to be done will depend on which ideas you have come up with and what matters most to your business, but we will start with some likely subjects, and you can customize the system to reflect your own circumstances. Here are some examples of idea tripwires.

## Idea tripwires

* How is this idea going to get done?
* Who is going to do it?
* By when?

Repeat this process for every idea. If the answer to any question is longer than one word, be suspicious of it. If it is longer than a sentence, it won't get done, so try again. If the answer to the second question is you, then write reminders in your personal organizer now to make sure it gets done. If the answer is someone other than you, get them to agree that they will, and put the same tripwires in their organizer.

The date by which it gets done needs careful thought. If you can trust yourself to meet a deadline, then great. If you can't, then put the necessary reminders in the way before it becomes time critical, and set yourself sanctions for missing your own timings. Don't fudge this. In his book *Simply Brilliant*, Fergus O'Connell points out that things either are or they aren't. In other words, they are either done or not done. So don't console yourself with unhelpful thoughts such as 'I'm halfway through it' or 'It's all in hand'. It is either finished, and ready to go public, or it isn't, and if it isn't, it's either late or useless.

**'To undertake is to achieve.'**

Emily Dickinson

Now set up your tripwires by getting up close and personal. Answer these questions and, crucially, enact right now the thing that will make sure it happens.

*6 set up your business tripwires and grenades*

## Personal planning tripwires

* What will make me get this done?
* Is that bulletproof, or too flimsy?
* Does that allow me to wriggle out of it later?
* If so, what sanction will force me to do it?
* Have I actually put that in place right now?

There is no room for excuses here because it is completely in your interests to get the thing done, even if it does lie a little way in the future. This technique works for specific items, but it also works for the overall shape of your business. If that is an exercise that you would find useful, then you might want to write down your one-year, three-year, five-year and ten-year aims. Actually, the time spans don't matter, but the principle does. Choose frequencies that are appropriate to your business, and write down the answers to these questions.

## Business planning tripwires

* What, ultimately, do I want for my business?
* By when?
* How exactly am I going to get there?
* Do I need help, and if so, from whom?
* Have I started yet?

**'The beginning is half of every action.'**

Greek proverb

Whoever the Greek person was, they had it right. The world is full of people who claim to have lots of ideas but, strangely, haven't quite started them. Do not allow yourself to be one of these people. Get started immediately, and learn as you go. You can always change your plan on the way, but don't fall into the trap of standing around pontificating when you could be using the time to get the thing done.

## *Dropping grenades in fishponds*

There is another technique that works for some people who need constant reminders to get organized and get stuff done. I call it dropping grenades in fishponds. The idea here is that you deliberately create cataclysmic circumstances in order to jolt yourself into doing the necessary thing. Some people need a severe shock to force them to do something, so here is a form of disaster planning that may help catapult you into action. We will call them grenades.

**Idea tripwires**

- How is this idea going to get done?
- Who is going to do it?
- By when?

**Personal planning tripwires**

- What will make me get this done?
- Is that bulletproof, or too flimsy?
- Does that allow me to wriggle out of it later?
- If so, what sanction will force me to do it?
- Have I actually put that in place right now?

**Business planning tripwires**

- What, ultimately, do I want for my business?
- By when?
- How exactly am I going to get there?
- Do I need help, and if so, from whom?
- Have I started yet?

*Tripwires checklist.*

> **Cataclysm** (noun): violent upheaval

The purpose of these questions is not to scare you senseless and prevent you from sleeping well. It is to scare up the important issues for those who bumble along for too long without actually getting done the bits that they know in their hearts will really make a difference.

## *Idea grenades*

* What if this were the only idea available?
* What if it never happened?
* What if there were 20 more like this?

You can see how this extreme line of questioning pushes everything that bit further. Go a bit over the top to test your mettle. If this were the only idea you had, would you still do it? There's no point in wasting time on tripwires and implementation if you aren't convinced, and if you aren't, then why should your colleagues or customers be?

## *Personal grenades*

* What if I could never work again?
* What if I took a year off?
* What if I quit this and did something totally different?

These are pretty poignant too, and the intention is to make you stop and think so that you can work out the severity of an item and how badly you want to do it. Then, if you conclude that it definitely does matter, you can engineer the necessary tripwires. We will investigate all this further in the next chapter when you write your Lifesmile Statement.

## *Business grenades*

* What if the business folded tomorrow?
* What if all the staff were fired?
* What if all our customers suddenly disappeared?

62    make your small business thrive

Nasty scorched earth scenarios like this are very polarizing and are good for helping you to clarify your thoughts so that you really know what you are trying to achieve. The principle is the same as for your personal issues. Use this Armageddon approach to determine how badly something matters, and how you are going to guarantee that it gets done.

---

**Idea grenades**

- What if this were the only idea available?
- What if it never happened?
- What if there were 20 more like this?

---

**Personal grenades**

- What if I could never work again?
- What if I took a year off?
- What if I quit this and did something totally different?

---

**Business grenades**

- What if the business folded tomorrow?
- What if all the staff were fired?
- What if all our cutomers suddenly disappeared?

---

*Grenades checklist.*

## Don't replace the original, replace the spare

We are working on the principle here that small reminders yield big results. It just depends how severe a memory jog you require, and only you can be the judge of that. If you are quite

**6 set up your business tripwires and grenades**     63

efficient, then you may not need any of these measures at all. If you have trouble with motivation, or you are a bit disorganized, then you may well do. Put the appropriate number of tripwires in place, but don't overdo it to the point that they are constantly preventing you from doing the task in hand. They are there to make you do things, not to stop you from doing them. If you put too many in place, you will be damming up the river to see how it flows, which would be pointless. Or, put another way, pulling the flowers up to see how they grow.

But there are also simple principles you can apply that save prevarication in your working day, week or year. One of my favourites is don't replace the original, replace the spare. Every good chef knows that you need a spare of everything, so that when you run out of the original, you simply reach for it, and the meal still happens. Many people in life never have a spare, so whenever they run out of something there is a panic. They then either rush about in a mad flap to buy another item, thus increasing their stress, or the meal doesn't happen. The analogy applies equally to those in business. Whether it is supplies or human resource, you always need a spare. When the spare is used up, buy another spare. Don't replace the original, replace the spare.

## Multitasking versus Rapid Sequential Tasking

Part of the knack of making sure things get done is realizing what you are actually capable of doing. Getting a lot done is often associated with multitasking, and there has been a lot of discussion about whether everyone is able to do it.

**Multitask** (verb): to work at several different tasks simultaneously

One theory suggests that women are far better at multitasking than men, and the evidence for that looks quite convincing. So if you are male and no good at multitasking, what can you do?

**64**   make your small business thrive

My suggestion is Rapid Sequential Tasking. If you can only do one thing at a time, then do it fast and move on to the next thing. Everyone has checklists, and they usually contain a curious mixture of important and trivial things to do. My research in scores of training sessions suggests that the average number of items on a checklist is between seven and 20. If it is less than seven, there is no need for a list, and if it is longer than 20, then the list is too demoralizing so the small things aren't added to it. So strip out the easy trivia from the important stuff, and rattle through it sequentially and quickly. Just because guys apparently can't 'do' multitasking, it doesn't mean they can't do Rapid Sequential Tasking.

## Put the effort in only where it gets you somewhere

Your ability to get stuff done is one thing. Whether you are doing the right stuff in the first place is a completely different matter. Any good business person will tell you that you need to develop the knack of working out whether you are pursuing the right opportunities, and deciding how much time and effort to spend on them. One of the hardest decisions to make is to pull out of something when you have invested a lot of physical and emotional energy into it. But pull out is precisely what you must do if the thing in question is going nowhere.

> *'If at first you don't succeed, try, try again. Then give up. No use being a damn fool about it.'*
>
> W. C. Fields

Try again by all means, and again. But don't keep repeating the same mistakes or misjudgements.

> *'The definition of insanity is doing the same thing over and over again and expecting different results.'*
>
> Benjamin Franklin

*set up your business tripwires and grenades*

65

You require a level of tenacity to get something done, and good judgement to decide when to retire gracefully. W. C. Fields suggests a fair bit of tenacity, coupled with the good sense to give up eventually when you have got nowhere.

> *'If at first you don't succeed, try, try again. Then use a stunt double.'*
>
> Arnold Schwarzenegger

That completes the setting up of your business tripwires, and possibly the detonation of some grenades. If you want to go into a lot more detail about how to get things done, look at my other book *Tick Achieve*. Now that you have worked out precisely what you want from your business, in the next chapter we will move on to identify what you want from your personal life.

## *Flashback*

* How have you arranged to trip yourself up?
* Over what time period?
* Have you put it in your personal organizer?
* Have you written it all down?
* What sanctions have you imposed on yourself?
* Have you resolved your idea, personal and business tripwires?
* Have you detonated your idea, personal and business grenades?
* Have you remembered to replace the spare, not the original?
* Are you a multitasker or a Rapid Sequential Tasker?
* Are you flogging any dead horses?

## Success Story: Richard Harrison, the information services Chief Executive who reinvented himself in pharmaceuticals

Sometimes you just have to sit back and admit that what you are currently doing isn't what you want. For some it happens at university when they begin a law degree and then move to modern languages. For others, it happens after they have experienced a first taste of working life in a traineeship. Worst of all, it happens when you are in your mid-30s, when you have responsibilities and have grown used to a substantial income.

That's when you have to reinvent yourself, and that's precisely what Richard did. After rising to the top in a large information services business, he became thoroughly bored and began to question whether he should be in the industry at all. He eventually decided to leave, but not before he had a cunning plan.

Actually, it wasn't that cunning. It would involve a heavy investment of cash, a lot of support from his partner and a large leap of faith. He would fund himself through business school and emerge equipped to run another type of business. He didn't know at this stage what type, and this was an uncertain element of his plan, but he knew he had to adapt to be happy in whatever work he chose to earn a living.

He discussed it with his wife, spoke to the bank, and rustled all his savings together. It was two years of hell. The work was hard and all consuming. It put a strain on his finances and his relationship. But he ploughed on through, completed the exams and passed. He had arrived on the other side – now what?

Throughout his study time, he had been on the lookout for a new potential field of business that he would enjoy, and he found one that took his fancy – pharmaceutical distribution. He had always been interested in healthcare delivery, and the privatization of many aspects of it had allowed him to design a business model that might work. He even made it the subject of his thesis.

Five years later, Richard had realized his ambition, and all because he had the bravery to reinvent himself.

*set up your business tripwires and grenades*

# 7

# *write your own Lifesmile Statement*

What am I like? Many people have never answered this question of themselves before. Take your time and be brutally honest. Everybody has a style, but you may never have paused to consider what it is. Now is the time to do it. Your personal style should dovetail perfectly with that of your business.

What do you really want? Your business should be a conduit for your personal aspirations. You can't reconcile the two unless you know what you really want. So make sure you know, and then you can do something about it. Try writing down your pledge. This could be to yourself, your business, your family or friends. Writing something down and pinning it on the wall has a polarizing effect. Live with your pledge and see if you can live up to it. Consolidate all the elements of your thinking into one powerful statement of intent.

As I mentioned earlier, there is no point in 'fixing' the business when you are not content yourself. So now we are going to force you to bare your soul (don't worry, you can do it in private if you want) so that you can accurately reconcile your working life with your personal wishes and aspirations. The process has five parts — four sets of questions you need to answer, and a concluding summary. So let's start.

## Part I: What am I like?

This is an exercise that I have often run in training sessions. Take a sheet of paper and write the question 'What am I like?' at the top. Take ten minutes or so to write down your thoughts. This is supposed to be an honest assessment of how you come across. You can produce a series of notes, or a flow of observations, so long as it is what you genuinely think you are like. If relevant, you can highlight distinctions between how you think you come across, and how you really feel. If you have trouble doing this, try these questions.

* If someone met you for the first time, how would they describe you?
* How would you describe yourself to someone you have never met?
* Are there differences between your work and outside personality?
* Is your inner self significantly different from your outward persona?

## Part II: Decide your own style

The previous exercise will have weeded out whether you are being unrealistic about yourself or not. If you have never thought about it before, you now have a description of yourself to consider. There may be elements of your style in it, or maybe not. If there aren't, or if you want to change how you come across, the next step is to define that style. Take another ten minutes to answer these questions.

* Who or what is your favourite person or team(s)?
* What qualities make them so good?
* How can those qualities inspire your approach?
* Now define your own personal style.

So now you have a personal assessment and a defined style in front of you. Put that aside for a moment. We will come back to it in a minute.

## Part III: So what do I really want?

So now we know what you are like, and what style you would like to emulate. Now let's get to the heart of what is going to make you happy in life. Answer these rather direct and personal questions on a separate sheet of paper.

* What's the point of my life?
* Why do I bother working?
* What, ultimately, do I want for myself?
* By when?

This needs to be a very honest exercise. There is no point in deluding yourself because you are the potential beneficiary, or loser, depending on how you reply. Your orientation should be 'I do this because ...'.

## Part IV: I pledge ...

Take another blank piece of paper and write at the top of it 'I pledge'. Now write down what you are going to do differently from now on in order to achieve what you want. If you can't articulate it in your own words, answer these three questions.

* How exactly am I going to get where I want to be?
* Do I need help and, if so, from whom?
* By when will I achieve this?

*7  write your own Lifesmile Statement*                    **71**

## Part V: My Lifesmile Statement

You have now effectively written all the elements of your Lifesmile Statement. It should have four parts so far, and we will now complete it with a fifth – the summary. Collect the four pieces of paper you should now have, and put them together. If you prefer, type them all out on one sheet along the lines shown in the figure below.

**1** This is what I am like
**2** This is my personal style
**3** What I really want is
**4** I pledge ...

All you have to do now is answer one final question.
**5** If there's one thing I am going to do it is ...

This completes your Lifesmile Statement. Everything on it is designed to make you happy, and if you manage to do what it says, you certainly will be. So print it out, blow it up large and stick it on the wall to remind yourself every day what you are all about.

---

**This is what I am like:**

_____

**This is my personal style:**

_____

**What I really want is:**

_____

**I pledge:**

_____

**If there's one thing I am going to do it is:**

_____

---

*My Lifesmile Statement.*

### Part I: What am I like?

- If someone met you for the first time, how would they describe you?
- How would you describe yourself to someone you have never met?
- Are there differences between your work and outside personality?
- Is your inner self significantly different from your outward persona?

### Part II: Decide your own style

- Who or what is your favourite person or team(s)?
- What qualities make them so good?
- How can those qualities inspire your approach?
- Now define your own personal style

### Part III: What do *really* want?

- What's the point of my life?
- Why do I bother working?
- What, ultimately, do I want for myself?
- By when?

### Part IV: I pledge …

- How exactly am I going to get where I want to be?
- Do I need help and, if so, from whom?
- By when will I achieve this?

### Part V: My Lifesmile Statement

- If there's one thing I am going to do it is:

*Complete Lifesmile Statement method.*

7 *write your own Lifesmile Statement*

## Try being angular

There are lots of ways to answer the questions we have just posed. If the answers come naturally to you, then move on to the next chapter or take a breather. These personal matters can be a bit harrowing sometimes. But if you developed writer's block, here are some suggestions to drag your opinions out of you. They are in there somewhere. You can try the same method that we used to determine the future of the business, by simply stating your one-year, three-year, five-year or ten-year aims for yourself. If not, be a bit more perverse. See if you agree or disagree with these assertions.

* To stay interesting, you have to stay angry.
* A happy owner means a good business.
* It is good to be conventionally odd.
* Big picture, small picture, forget the picture – it doesn't matter.
* Never apologize, never explain.

If you agree, write down why, and how you personally enact that approach. If you disagree, write down why, plus your alternative.

**'I'm always doing things I can't do. That's how I get to do them.'**

Pablo Picasso

Push yourself to have aspirations that are beyond what you currently do. It keeps you stimulated and increases your chances of success when you are growing your business, because interested students are more tenacious about their subject. In short, consider doing some things you have never done.

## A board meeting with yourself

Another way of dealing with writer's block is to imagine having a board meeting with yourself. Of course, self-employed people do this all the time, and they are very used to mulling over conflicting thoughts on their own. It is a technique you can use when you have lots of colleagues too. Imagine you are in a board meeting, and that you are being subjected to intense questioning. Take the nastiest questions that you didn't fancy answering from the process in this chapter, and pretend that you absolutely have to answer. If you still can't produce anything, ask a partner, close friend, or someone who knows nothing about your business, to force you to answer them.

> **'A fanatic is one who can't change his mind and won't change the subject.'**
>
> Winston Churchill

## Nailing a jelly to the wall

An exasperated colleague of mine once exclaimed: 'I'm trying to nail a jelly to the wall here.' Bear in mind that if something is vague, it's useless, so you must have clear statements about what you desire for your future. Keep it clear and keep it fresh.

> **'When you've run out of red, use blue!'**
>
> Pablo Picasso

You have now completed the tripwires that should have secured what you need to achieve on behalf of the business, and the Lifesmile Statement has articulated what you want as an individual. We could stop there, and by all means do. There is, however, always the small matter of the unexpected, lurking around every corner, to scupper even the best-laid plans. So, if you fancy it, read the next two chapters.

## Flashback

* Have you clarified what you are like?
* Have you decided your own style?
* Have you written down what you really want?
* Have you made some pledges?
* If so, what are they?
* Have you completed your Lifesmile Statement?
* Have you tried some new angles?
* Are you able to have a board meeting with yourself?
* Is your plan clear and fresh?
* Are you ready to pin it on the wall?

*7 write your own Lifesmile Statement*

# 8

# *don't confuse movement with progress*

76  make your small business thrive

Some people love to look busy, but often what they are doing has no bearing on the matter in hand. Concentrate on sensible action rather than generating activity for the sake of it. Generating huge amounts of stuff (output) may have nothing to do with the end result (outcome). So before you produce endless documents and spreadsheets, work out your desired outcome and work backwards from there. Are you making something more complicated than it needs to be? If so, stop it. Businesses don't actually have to be busy. A certain amount of work, judiciously undertaken for the right price, could liberate weeks of free time. You don't have to be Nostradamus to predict most things that will happen to your business in the next week, month or year. So work out what those things are and make plans so that you are not caught by surprise.

Much ado about nothing. Lots of movement but no forward motion. All talk and no action. How many times have you observed in life that a lot appears to be happening, but in fact, nothing much really is? That is what this chapter is all about. If you run a business, or wish to grow one successfully, then you haven't got the time, nor probably the patience, to allow people to faff about, or events to drift along, when what they are doing has no particular bearing on the main point. It is what the Italians call the English Disease: rushing around creating the *impression* that things are happening, but with no real tangible results.

Before I continue, I need to acknowledge the inspiration behind the chapter's title. My brother has a friend who is an experienced diplomat. They were driving on the motorway one day when an overtaking car sped rapidly into a gap just in front of them. The diplomat, an experienced pilot as well as a highly competent driver, declared: 'Don't confuse movement with progress.' The moral lies in an ability to move towards the intended objective without undue histrionics which, although they create the impression of activity, have no true bearing on the ultimate outcome. This is a vital lesson for anyone in business. Let's have a look at some other ways of phrasing it.

* Commando raids are good. Carpet bombing isn't.
* Laser strikes are good. Detonating everything isn't.
* Specific things are good. Generating lots of stuff to do isn't.
* Orderly progress to an intended destination is good. Buzzing around like a fly in a bottle isn't.
* It is better to arrive quietly than to make a big noise trying to get there.

This last one sounds like an ancient Chinese proverb, but it isn't. I just made it up. But you get the idea. Do not allow yourself to be fooled by a smokescreen of activity when you know very well it is simply to disguise the fact that the main item is not being done.

## Action not activity

A lot of modern business people think that they are really clever if they are busy. I disagree. The smart operator knows how to have things working for them. What's so clever about being busy? All you need is a certain amount of activity to keep you stimulated, leaving the remainder of the time for you to pursue the things that really matter to you. Any fool can appear to be permanently busy. If you ring someone for an appointment and they can offer you a 'window of opportunity' in six months' time, then there are two possible explanations. The first is that they are hugely in demand, and thoroughly enjoying every second of it. In which case, good luck to them. The second (more likely) reason is that they are not in control of their own life and have too many meetings discussing stuff that doesn't have much bearing on the main point. Which applies to you?

From the training sessions that I have run over the past few years, I have learnt that the average amount of time that people in service industries spend bogged down in meetings is between 40 and 80 per cent of their working week. This figure is staggering. When you consider that the majority of meetings are to discuss how to move something forward, this statistic begs the question of when exactly these people are supposed to find the time to enact all the things that are raised in these apparently highly important meetings. If you want something to happen, concentrate on the action, not on activity that makes it look as though action is occurring.

## Outcome not output

Meetings are not the only culprit in this context. In many corporations, bureaucracy is endemic. So often they make it look as though something is happening, when frequently it isn't. The output of an organization really doesn't matter much. It is the outcome that matters. If you achieve something excellent, who cares how you got there? If you have a great idea, who cares whether it happened in a flash, or over two weeks, or several years?

*8 don't confuse movement with progress*

Can you imagine someone saying: 'What a great idea. I wonder how many meetings they needed to make that happen?' I don't think so. Here is a list of business activities that, more often than not, are a waste of time.

* Meetings
* Conference calls
* Status reports
* Reports
* Travelling
* Communal emails

I can hear you exclaiming now. He is completely wrong! We couldn't function without these things! But look again, and you will see that I have said 'more often than not'. This is the point. With some careful thought and application, you should be able to reduce your output by half, so that you can concentrate on the outcome. Try asking yourself some of these questions.

* Do I really need to have that meeting?
* Does it need to be that long?
* Do all those people need to be there?
* Do I need this piece of paperwork?
* Does anyone else?
* Does that need to be written down?
* Do I need to send that email?
* Do I need to have that conversation?
* Does that even need to be discussed?

There are hundreds of questions that can change your working life. In Chapter 5, we looked at Lee Iacocca's quote: 'They tell me what they think. Then I decide.' If you are good at business, you weigh up the situation, make a decision, and then get on with it. It can save hours, days, even years of hanging about. So the best question of all is:

* Can we just get on with it?

This question will blow the doors off most government departments and have millions of big corporate citizens dashing to their subsidized canteens for a cheap cappuccino. For many more questions like this, read my other book *So What?* You see, most people *want* to look busy, regardless of whether there is an outcome. Don't let that person be you.

## Spotting obfuscation

There will be plenty reading this who will think that the author has gone a bit barmy at this point, but bear with me. Have you ever heard of obfuscation?

> **Obfuscation** (noun): the act or an instance of making something deliberately obscure or difficult to understand

It's not quite the same as time wasting. It is nothing to do with being idle or unintelligent. No, it is much smarter than that. It is about making something appear more complicated than it truly is, or needs to be. Lots of professions do it all the time. People have to hire lawyers because they have surrounded themselves with a language that no one else can understand. City traders are the same. Most industries have a jargon that provides a force field that is designed to exclude everyone else. That enables them to appear clever, and to cast a veil over their activities. That in turn allows them to charge more for their services and generally feel superior. All industries do it. It isn't even a particularly evil activity. It seems to happen naturally. You know the kind of thing.

> *'Jane was talking to Dave about the ZXC. Of course, he said it was ludicrous that the project manager never filled in the 87-K, and now that LOD have got hold of it, it'll probably be sent to the pit bulls in back-end architecture or thrown into the hands of AWOB with the rest of the ideas from Project Azalea.'*

Impenetrable rubbish, I am sure you will agree. Under no circumstances should you ever end up talking like this. It undermines your credibility and makes you sound less intelligent than you are. If you remain unconvinced that there is too much language in business

*8 don't confuse movement with progress*

that encourages confusion, have a look at the range of phrases in use to describe unnecessary talk.

> **Blather** (Scottish; blether): foolish talk; nonsense
> **Drivel:** unintelligible language
> **Hot air:** empty talk
> **Jabber:** to speak without making sense
> **Nonsense:** something that makes no sense
> **Piffle:** nonsense
> **Rabbit:** to talk inconsequentially
> **Static:** interference in transmissions
> **Verbiage:** excessive and often meaningless use of words
> **Waffle:** to speak in a vague and wordy manner
> **Whim-wham:** something fanciful; a trifle
> **White noise:** sound with wide continuous range of frequencies of uniform intensity

I have barely scratched the surface. The list goes on and on, and the descriptive vocabulary for this phenomenon is so rich precisely *because* it is such a frequent occurrence. But be under no illusion: if you want to get something done, you haven't got time for this sort of prevarication. Life is not that complicated, and business certainly doesn't have to be.

> **'There cannot be a crisis next week. My schedule is already full.'**
>
> Henry Kissinger

You will have heard the axiom that work expands to fit the time available in which to do it. The alternative, of course, is that you are too busy to create the time for anything else. Neither extreme makes any sense. Why surround yourself with irrelevant things to do, when you have lots of other genuinely interesting things to do? Something of a rhetorical question perhaps, but we all have examples of circumstances in which nothing important is getting done because too much irrelevant stuff is being done instead. If you suspect that this might be the case with your business, or with any of your customers, then you have some serious thinking to do.

## Business does not mean being busy

Busy used to mean (literally) being actively or fully engaged, and there's nothing wrong with that. But it has also come to mean overcrowded with detail, and that is not a good thing. Never confuse movement with progress. Work out the bits that matter, and do them only. If you have spare time, do something you want to do in order to ensure your sustained happiness, not something that supports the idea that you are frantically busy. Try these phrases to puncture the idea that being busy is beneficial.

* Claiming to be too busy is the last refuge of an ailing business person.
* Being busy used to be macho — now it is gender neutral.
* If you are too busy, you have no time for yourself.
* If you are too busy, you have no time for anyone else.
* If you are too busy, you are one-dimensional.
* If you are too busy, you are missing the point.
* If you are too busy, you are missing out on life.
* If you are too busy, you are incompetent.

## There's a tidal wave coming. Here's a paper cup

Many people in business feel that they are under-equipped to deal with what life is going to throw at them. They feel as though they have been given a paper cup, and told that there is a tidal wave coming. But coping with business, or 'busyness', is all about guessing the landscape and the possible outcomes before they occur. This is not nearly as difficult as you might think. The first step is to realize that things may well go wrong before they go wrong. That's not a particularly complicated idea now is it? Put even more simply, assume the worst, and do your best. Life's a mess. Adapt.

*8 don't confuse movement with progress*

Be prepared for changes and make it up as you go along. Plan B is often better than Plan A. (The idea of plan B being more productive than plan A is discussed in another of my books, *Run Your Own Business*.) Stick to the simple stuff, and don't let administration and bureaucracy get in the way. If you view business as a nasty tidal wave, then your perspective needs some adjustment. Try asking yourself these questions.

* What is likely to happen?
* When?
* What can I do to anticipate that?
* What can I do to prepare for that?
* What can I do to influence that?
* What can I do to prevent that?
* What can I do to make that tolerable?

It is a form of disaster planning, except that these are not disasters. They are just the normal nuisances that happen in business every day.

> *'A change of nuisances is as good as a holiday.'*
>
> David Lloyd George

## Everything busier than everything else

Don't confuse movement with progress. The illusion that things will be better when they are busier needs careful consideration, because it doesn't make any sense. Do you really agree with the idea that if there is a lot happening, then progress is being made? The old joke goes that when marketing activity does not have the desired effect, marketing directors immediately do more of it. Instead, they would be better placed to work out why it didn't work first, and then make their next move. What do politicians do when they see light at the end of the tunnel? Order more tunnel! So before you rush around like a headless chicken without knowing why, ask yourself these questions.

* Why am I doing this?
* What's wrong with things as they are?
* Will the proposed activity get me anywhere?

* Is this worth doing?
* Why?
* What is the likely return in relation to my efforts?
* Is this the beginning, the middle or the end of the sequence?
* Do I need to rethink this?

At the heart of all this is the maxim: Never do anything unless you know why you are doing it. No one is proposing that you become idle – simply that you do not fool yourself into believing that all the rushing around you are doing is achieving anything, unless of course you have genuinely worked out that it definitely is. In which case, move on to the next chapter immediately.

## *Flashback*

* Have you confused movement with progress?
* Have you banished activity in favour of action?
* Can you spot obfuscation?
* If so, what have you done to eradicate it?
* Have you reduced the amount of bureaucracy in your life?
* Have you asked why you can't just get on with it?
* Do you often claim to be too busy?
* Is it really true?
* Have you anticipated what is likely to happen before it does?
* Ask again: why am I doing this?

# corporations don't have memories

History does not repeat itself. We often learn very little from the past, as constant boom and bust cycles demonstrate. Don't assume that what has happened before will happen again, or continue to happen. The relationships that you have in business may not really be relationships. They may be passing involvements. So it is important that you are involved with many customers on many fronts. Corporations are just clusters of individuals, so if you think you have a relationship with a corporation, think again. Try to make your association with corporations as broad and deep as possible. If a corporation isn't interested in what you have to offer then you have two choices: try a new angle or move on to another one. It's that simple.

# History does not repeat itself

There is a common notion that history often repeats itself. Shirley Bassey certainly sang about it at length, but I think that it is nonsense. As a species, man has a spectacular track record of 'unlearning' all sorts of skills. You only have to look at a few ancient civilizations to spot that. So information and knowledge is by no means always passed down, and that can cause all sorts of problems for businesses that desire a long-term relationship with a particular customer.

> *'History does not repeat itself. At best it sometimes rhymes.'*
>
> Mark Twain

Of course, similar things do happen over time. But is this because people have deliberately engineered it, or because they are making the same mistakes another time? Part of the problem revolves around the manner in which history is recorded. We all know that politicians, military men, writers and so on all like to express events on their own terms, and people in business do it too. In Chapter 4, we discussed the idea that you should always admit if something was a fluke, otherwise you would delude yourself into thinking that you had orchestrated the success. Well, people in business love rewriting history too. That's because it makes them look better. If you want a pay rise, then summarize the last couple of years as a relentless period of progress, and you may well get one. Everyone likes to make it look as though they made clinical strategic decisions to influence a situation for the better, when frequently those things were going to happen anyway.

> *'History is not what you thought. It is what you can remember.'*
>
> W. C. Sellar

So history can easily be rewritten and, often, it is rewritten in front of your very eyes. This may or may not bother you in a global context, but it might if it refers to business issues that have

**88** make your small business thrive

a deep and immediate bearing on your welfare and happiness. Let's take an example. You or your company starts working for a large corporation with, say, more than 3,000 staff. You have a main contact, in charge of procurement, and get to meet three or four other less senior characters as you work on the first project. That goes well, so over the next three years you win more and more work, to the point where this customer accounts for 65 per cent of your income, and 60 per cent of your profit. All is seemingly rosy, but then things start to happen. Your main contact is moving on. They might have been fired. They might be retiring. They might be moving to another division, or overseas. The reason doesn't matter. They remain a great fan of you and your work, but they aren't there any more to sign off the money. For a while, there is no replacement. Their subordinates can authorize a limited amount of other work, but the main stuff is put on hold until a successor arrives. One of the team goes on maternity leave. The successor arrives, and won't take a meeting with you because they have too much else to do, and you have never met before. They bring in their own team and start working with someone else. Without so much as a conversation, you have lost two-thirds of your business.

## _Corporations: just clusters of individuals_

Time was, you took your job as a trainee at the bank, and 50 years later you collected your commemorative gold watch at your retirement bash. Not any more. People come and go with alarming regularity, and that means your customers can move at the same speed, because they are effectively the same people. In marketing, the average length of time that someone spends in a job is 18 months. This is just enough time to:
* fail to understand the job properly
* deny all responsibility for previous events
* initiate a few things on scanty information
* leave before they are finished, thereby avoiding responsibility for any outcome.

_9 corporations don't have memories_

I exaggerate to make a point, but you get the idea. Now translate this from a personal level to the one that could affect the relationship between your company and theirs. Your new customer may only be around long enough to:

* grasp a vague notion of what you do
* put a few things in train with your company
* fail to inform colleagues of the extent of your capabilities
* move on to somewhere else.

That is a chain of events that could occur even with the best will and the most decent person in the world. It's not personal – it's just business. Even worse, their successor could:

* fail to understand what you do properly
* show disinterest in all previous work
* not bother to take a meeting with you
* use previous contacts to replace you for similar work
* unwittingly destroy your business.

## Your relationships aren't

So you are faced with the constantly moving customer. Once you have got the hang of this, you will be forced to admit that your relationships aren't.

**'Firings will continue until morale improves.'**

Anonymous

People are cheap these days, and loyalty is a rare thing. They get fired, you get fired. It's as simple as that. Many people running businesses reckon that they are only one phone call away from disaster. If the call comes, they are going to be making redundancies or folding the business. So let's have a look at some of the things that can be done to alleviate this sort of problem when it arises, as it inevitably will one day.

## Overcoming corporate amnesia

'Sorry, who are you?' You can hear the phone call now, and it won't be that pleasant. Your major customer doesn't know who you are. So how do you ingratiate yourself so that they do remain a customer? Here are some ideas.

* **Be more organized than they are.** When people arrive new in a job, it is difficult for them to know what to do next. If you are efficient and well organized, you can become very useful to them and help them along. Let them know how, and look for an opportunity to prove it.
* **Keep records.** In certain businesses, customers have no idea where their predecessor kept the information on a certain subject. Frequently, knowledge is lost on the way. If you have it, you need to let them know, and use your knowledge of their business to your advantage. History may not repeat itself, but something will have been learnt on the way.
* **Anticipate seasonal variations.** A lot of businesses are seasonal, which means that contact with customers could be scarce in the low season. If this applies to your business, then anticipate the periods of minimal contact, and do something about it. For example, if you conduct business with them intensively over the summer, then deliberately arrange to meet in December to stay in touch.
* **Use case histories.** Write up and analyse the success and value of what you have already done for the customer. Quantify it. Show where improvements can be made. Then add lots of new ideas.

*'Nothing has really happened until it has been described.'*

Virginia Woolf

## Overcoming corporate apathy

Let's say that the customer hasn't forgotten who you are. Instead, they are indifferent about hearing what you have to offer. Try some of these approaches.

* **Rip it up and start again.** Pretend you have never had this customer, and start again. Use all the enthusiasm of a new

kid on the block, attack the subject with a new perspective, and propose a meeting to reveal it all.

* **Reinvent yourself.** It is of course possible that you personally are a bit jaded when it comes to this customer. If that is true, then consider introducing a colleague to the mix to replicate the conditions of a new relationship.
* **Do something imaginative.** Introduce fresh ideas. Do not attach yourself too heavily to the past. The new person doesn't care what went on before, unless it has a direct bearing on their fortunes now. In which case, tell them straightaway what worked previously, but do remember that the past is not very interesting to most people in business. It is the future that they are worried about.

*'Never let yesterday use up too much of today.'*

Will Rogers

## Flashback

* Have you learnt anything from the past?
* How are you going to apply that learning?
* Are you guilty of rewriting history?
* Have you anticipated relationships that could go wrong?
* What have you done about that?
* Have you considered ways to overcome corporate amnesia or apathy?
* Are you more organized than your customers?
* Are you capable of reinventing yourself?
* Are you honest about yourself in relation to the competition?
* Have you been totally objective about past performance?